Remembering
Daytona Beach

Harold D. Cardwell, Sr.

TURNER
PUBLISHING COMPANY

Road-beach racing resumed after a hiatus caused by World War II. The track was laid out for 3.5 miles (half the course was on the beach and half on the hard pavement) having a north turn and a south turn. The approach from the beach was hard-packed marl and shell.

Remembering
Daytona Beach

Turner Publishing Company
www.turnerpublishing.com

Remembering Daytona Beach

Copyright © 2010 Turner Publishing Company

Library of Congress Control Number: 2010923495

ISBN: 978-1-59652-625-9

Printed in the United States of America

ISBN: 978-1-68336-825-0 (-pbk.)

CONTENTS

ACKNOWLEDGMENTS VII

PREFACE VIII

FROM THE WILDERNESS TO A TOWN
    (1880s–1906) 1

TRANSPORTATION, INDUSTRY, AND WORLD WAR I
    (1907–1918) 39

REAL ESTATE BOOM, DEPRESSION, AND WORLD WAR II
    (1919–1945) 75

GROWTH, THE BEACH, TOURISM, AND RACING
    (1946–1949) 113

NOTES ON THE PHOTOGRAPHS 132

Tex Madsen, over 7 feet tall and from Texas, at one time ran a photography concession on the beach. For a small fee, beachgoers could sit astride a saddle on the back of Ferdinand the Bull and have their picture taken. His wife, Verna, continued the enterprise after her husband's death.

ACKNOWLEDGMENTS

This volume, *Remembering Daytona Beach,* is the result of the cooperation and efforts of many individuals and organizations. It is with great thanks that we acknowledge in particular the generous assistance of the State Archives of Florida.

We would also like to thank the following individuals for valuable contributions and assistance in making this work possible:

Harold D. Cardwell, Sr., our writer

N. Adam Watson, Photographic Archivist, State Archives of Florida

PREFACE

Daytona Beach has thousands of historic photographs that reside in archives, both locally and nationally. This book began with the observation that, while those photographs are of great interest to many, they are not easily accessible. During a time when Daytona Beach is looking ahead and evaluating its future course, many people are asking, How do we treat the past? These decisions affect every aspect of the city—architecture, public spaces, commerce, infrastructure—and these, in turn, affect the way that people live their lives. This book seeks to provide easy access to a valuable, objective look into the history of Daytona Beach.

The power of photographs is that they are less subjective than words in their treatment of history. Although the photographer can make subjective decisions regarding subject matter and how to capture and present it, photographs seldom interpret the past to the extent textual histories can. For this reason, photography is uniquely positioned to offer an original, untainted look at the past, allowing the viewer to learn for himself what the world was like a century or more ago.

This project represents countless hours of review and research. The researchers and writer have reviewed thousands of photographs in numerous archives. We greatly appreciate the generous assistance of the individuals and organizations listed in the acknowledgments of this work, without whom this project could not have been completed.

The goal in publishing this work is to provide broader access to this set of extraordinary photographs that seek to inspire, provide perspective, and evoke insight that might assist people who are responsible for determining the future of Daytona Beach. In addition, the book seeks to preserve the past with adequate respect and reverence.

With the exception of touching up imperfections that have accrued with the passage of time and cropping where necessary, no changes have been made. The focus and clarity of many images are limited to the technology and the ability of the photographer at the time they were recorded.

The work is divided into eras. Beginning with some of the earliest known photographs of Daytona Beach, the first section records photographs through the beginning of the twentieth century. The second section covers the early twentieth century through the World War I era. Section Three spans a period of time from the close of the First World War to the close of the Second. The last section moves into the postwar era.

In each of these sections we have made an effort to capture various aspects of life through our selection of photographs. People, commerce, transportation, infrastructure, religious institutions, and educational institutions have been included to provide a broad perspective.

We encourage readers to reflect as they go walking in Daytona Beach, strolling through the city, its parks, and its neighborhoods. It is the publisher's hope that in utilizing this work, longtime residents will learn something new and that new residents will gain a perspective on where Daytona Beach has been, so that each can contribute to its future.

—*Todd Bottorff, Publisher*

This primitive log structure was one of the earliest landmarks along the Halifax riverfront that later became Daytona. It stood about where 154 South Beach Street is today. The logs were hand-hewn and boards were hand split. Later on, rough-sawn lumber was available to build houses when a sawmill was built in the settlement.

FROM THE WILDERNESS TO A TOWN

(1880s–1906)

The St. Johns and Halifax River Railway Company brought the narrow-gauge railroad to Daytona, December 2, 1886. The steam-powered locomotive, *Bulow,* was built by the Baldwin Railroad Works. Pulling the first cars with passengers to the terminal at Daytona's riverfront, it introduced a new era of transportation to the settlement.

Workers are seen here doing the grading of the right of way for Ocean Boulevard. Mrs. Helen Wilmans Post, riding in her carriage, inspects the construction work. Later the Wilmans Post Opera House and hotel were built on this new boulevard, which became Seabreeze Boulevard.

This fashionable vernacular two-story frame home with gable roof stood on Ridgewood Avenue. New houses were being built in this section of town. This photograph was taken by E. G. Harris, well-known author and photographer.

This early photograph by E. G. Harris shows bathers on the beach and in the water. In the background are new buildings and hotels, which were beginning to dot the landscape. The beachside was being developed.

The Yacht Club was chartered in 1896. In this view, log pilings are being driven in preparation for its construction. A new, modern clubhouse was completed in 2006. The old structure was to be dismantled in 2007 because of environmental damage to the waterfront.

A nineteenth-century version of a day at the beach—horses, carriages, and people in full dress take in the view. The Keating Pier can be seen in the background. By the turn of the century, the pier had been destroyed by storms.

The new, fashionable yacht club is visible to the right. Also pictured is the river pier for unloading and shipping supplies by steamboat. Sabal palms and oak trees line the road.

This automobile was owned by H. H. Seelye, who helped form an auto club. In 1903, the Florida East Coast Automobile Association was organized. The club was responsible for promoting races on the beach. This photograph was taken after 1898, in front of the Colonnades Hotel, Ocean Boulevard.

The South Bridge was a great achievement for Daytona. This bridge enabled horse and carriage and later the horseless carriage to cross from the peninsula to the mainland. The bridge tender's house is visible at the draw and in the distance the Halifax River Yacht Club and Palmetto House.

Palmetto House accommodated new settlers and workers who came to live and work in the new town. This hotel was advantageous to fishermen, who could leave in boats nearby for a daily catch, and hunters, who could retreat into the backwoods for a day of hunting deer and turkey. Mary Hoag was manager and proprietor.

Wind-sailors, bicycles, steam-powered, gas-powered, and human-powered vehicles gather at the beach for E. G. Harris to make this impressive photograph. A lone horse and buggy stands apart in the distance, as though to suggest its passage into history.

The jitney, pictured here, was a forerunner of the city bus. It brought passengers from the depot to hotels or for sightseeing tours or shopping. Canvas tops were later added to protect riders from inclement weather.

The prominent lady dressed in a blouse and long skirt below was the wife of Henry K. DuBois, a well-known physician of Port Orange.

This early photograph shows buildings along an unpaved South Beach Street. In the distance a horse-drawn enclosed wagon delivers supplies. In the foreground is a barbershop and the City Hotel.

D. D. Rogers, civil engineer, was well known throughout Florida as a land surveyor. It was appropriate that these engineers hold their convention at Daytona. The Florida East Coast Railway offered the best transportation at that time for them to attend.

This wooden pier gave fishermen and tourists a chance to catch fish. Occasionally they got a big one to photograph and show their northern friends. Sightseers could stroll out on the pier to breathe the salt air and in summer to cool off in the sea breezes.

Daytona had a busy railroad station. Tourists coming from the north to stay in sunny Florida brought their bags and trunks to stay at homes and hotels during the winter season. Horse-drawn carriages and wagons could be obtained from a nearby livery stable.

Helen Wilmans Post published her mental science paper *Freedom* on the ground floor of the opera house seen here. Colonel and Mrs. C. C. Post developed Ocean Boulevard with hotels, stores, a post office, and cultural events in the opera house. They platted the town of Seabreeze, which she called the City Beautiful.

Buildings on Ocean Boulevard in this view looking west are the Clarendon Inn, several homes, the Shell House (later the Geneva Hotel), and the Wilmans Opera House. Near the river stood the Colonnades Hotel.

Visible at lower-left on this tree-lined avenue, a stone step serves as a horse carriage stop, enabling passengers to step into a carriage or wagon. A homeowner poses with his bicycle.

This launch moored at a dock on north Beach Street ferried passengers across the river to a landing near today's Main Street. Captain L. E. Ellenwood operated the *Dixie* for several years from the mainland to the peninsula. He was owner from 1903 to 1913. Tokens were used for fare and could be purchased in advance of boarding.

The first building at left was Burdine's Pharmacy. Hitching posts for horses are visible on the unpaved street. In a few years, masonry buildings would replace wooden and old Beach Street would take on a new look.

The *Cherokee* launch prepares to leave its dock. This boat took passengers and freight as far north as the Tomoka River and south to New Smyrna. The first city hall and fire station are visible in the background.

The *Uncle Sam* made daily trips to Tomoka and three times a week to New Smyrna. This boat carried passengers and light freight. It also conducted scenic tours for tourists on the Halifax and Tomoka rivers.

To the left is Daytona's lumberyard, which later became City Island. On the right midway across is the city jail. Across the bridge to the left, just visible, is the Lawrence Thompson home and to the right James N. Gamble's home. This route led east to the Atlantic Ocean and today is known as Silver Beach Avenue.

Tourists and visitors at the beach enjoy themselves on a pleasant day. Here a single horseless carriage sputters along, wending its way through the milling crowd.

In this image tourists and townspeople have come out to watch two sport racers, just visible in the distance.

This estate covered most of the block surrounded by Beach Street, Bay Street, and Palmetto Avenue. The Queen Anne mansion, enclosed by a stout rock wall, was home to Mr. Burgoyne, a retired printer from New York City. He died in 1916 and the mansion was demolished in 1941 to make way for a new shopping area along Beach Street.

This boat is moored at a dock north of City Island. The Public Library and City Jail are visible to the right. To handle well, the sailboat required skill, especially during races, and was a common sight on the river.

Logging employed teamsters to snake logs up a ramp and onto high wheels, for pulling by oxen overland to a sawmill. The teamster had to be well trained in handling the oxen and the load of logs. Heavy loads frequently made ruts in the road.

This odd assortment of early automobiles forms a line on the beach January 14, 1905, near Ormond Beach and the Flying Mile. Speed seconds were calculated for the measured mile.

Mary McLeod Bethune started her school teaching five girls. She taught them to work with their hands and improve their social skills. She was able to persuade the industrialists who lived in Daytona in the winter and local businessmen to assist her with funds and supplies, the result of which was a flourishing school. Those contributing included James N. Gamble, Thomas White, H. D. Rhodes, and Lawrence Thompson, as well as other local citizens.

Beach Street as seen from atop adjoining boat house. Ellenwood's dock and landing are visible in the foreground. Captain L. E. Ellenwood was owner of the ferry from 1903 to 1913. Facing an unpaved Beach Street are various businesses. On the riverfront are clusters of sabal palms. In the distance is the former Florida East Coast Railway Depot, which became the city hall. Nearby is the city jail.

Daytona has always been associated with auto racing, but early time trials were held in Ormond through the flying mile area of the beach. As cars became faster they had to use the full length of the beach at Ormond, extending runs through Daytona's beach. Arthur MacDonald, pictured here, has an English-built, six-cylinder, 90-horsepower Napier. His record speed was 104.651 M.P.H.

In this view north, on the left is Burdine's Pharmacy, and in the distance the Hotel Despland is visible.

Turpentine was one of the most important products of the pine forest near Daytona. Mr. Paxton shipped turpentine and rosin to Savannah, Georgia. He was manager of the entire operation including the commissary, barrel making, and the living quarters for the workers. Paxton worked for many years at the naval stores operation.

Today this bridge is called the Main Street Bridge—the main entrance to the ocean beach. Women in long skirts, cyclists, and pedestrians all stop to pose for the photographer, but a little dog has more important business on the agenda.

Transportation, Industry, and World War I

(1907–1918)

Dressed in attire appropriate for autumn, three generations of one family gather on the beach to pose for the photographer while team and driver wait nearby.

This was a typical street scene in Daytona when pedestrians gathered at a store or a boarding home. The organ grinder depended on gratuities for his living. The monkey often held a cup for loose coins. The two women are being entertained by the well-kept monkey.

Left to right are Ed Lindberg, oiler; George Young, engineer; and Chief Messmore, superintendent, standing in front of a new generator installed to make possible electric lighting. In the beginning, electricity was available only for an allotted number of hours. Many facilities had to close late at night.

These whales, 35 to 40 feet long, washed ashore along the beach south of Daytona. Using the giant kettles from the Dunlawton Sugar Mill. Frank Sams, Albert Moeller, Elmer Oliver, Jerome Maley, John Pettigrew, and Captain S. Bennett partnered to chop up these sea creatures and make whale oil. Their method failed.

This large, well-known inn was home to many winter visitors. Some guests came back to the same room each year. Standing at the northeast corner of Palmetto and Ivy Lane for many years, the inn was eventually demolished to widen Palmetto Avenue.

This boat once plied the waters of the Halifax River. A steam-powered craft with two decks and a pilot house in front on top, it featured an open area for entertaining guests.

This outstanding home was on Ridgewood Avenue and encompassed several architectural styles, mostly Classical Revival. Masonry walls are hand-formed block made in molds. Artistic porch railings and columns adorn the front and side elevations. A sun room with chimney is at the side.

The Keating pier was the forerunner of the Main Street Pier today. The hexagon-towered house with porch was reported to be Charles Burgoyne's beach house. To the north in front of the old Claradon Inn was the Port Pier, which was destroyed many years ago by a northeaster storm. Often these storms did as much damage as a hurricane along the oceanfront.

This crowded depot loading area was awaiting the unloading of luggage and steamer trunks. Tourists brought all of their clothing and accessories for the winter when they arrived in town.

Harry B. Shefts in his Hotchkiss racer participates in a day at the races, March 5, 1908. Time trials and individual races used the full length of the beach from Ormond to Daytona.

A disastrous fire leaves enough time for guests and hotel workers to remove personal belongings. Furnishings were stored at nearby homes. The belongings of some guests were taken to the beach for safety.

These bathers appear to be enjoying the surf in their store-bought wool bathing suits. The lady at right sports a nautical collar, wool skirt, and leg covers. Both women are wearing shoes.

When young ladies came to the beach and stayed in hotels, they always had a chaperone. Parasols offered protection against the sun. This photograph was taken near the beach pier on a sand dune.

Visitors to the city founded by Matthias Day take an afternoon stroll on an unpaved Loomis Avenue named for Matthias's son, Loomis Day.

The Halifax Yacht Club was a place to see and to be seen. If you were the commodore, you were the most prestigious person in town. Membership comprised city officials and businessmen who frequently met for lunch to promote Daytona. Here various types of boats are moored at the club's dock.

Each winter Charles Burgoyne paid for a band to play concerts in the special gazebo built for entertainment. People came from near and far just to hear this band. A variety of music was played, including martial music, today known as parade music.

Famed aviator Glenn Curtiss came to Ormond and Daytona many times. Businessmen paid Curtiss $3,500 for his pilot, John A. D. McCurdy, to make three flights off the sands of Daytona Beach. Curtiss's early craft, shown here, features a rather bulky-looking water-cooled engine.

Passengers await the ferry at the landing to cross the Halifax River to beachside. Captain Ellenwood was always on schedule and reputedly very polite to his passengers. Roundtrip tokens were available in advance for the return to the west side in downtown Daytona.

The first bridge to cross the Halifax was great news for people building homes on the beachside. Lumber and other materials no longer needed ferrying. Here townspeople ride and stroll, taking advantage of the river breezes.

This clubhouse was constructed for the Elks at the northwest corner of Volusia and Palmetto. Featuring brick masonry construction and columns on the front, this building stood for many years at this location.

In a neat and tidy kitchen, Mary Bethune, the lady dressed in black, instructs her students in how to prepare food. This is the earliest image of the interior of Faith Hall (ca. 1912).

At one time, an electric trolley crossed Daytona's concrete bridge and went all the way over to the peninsula to what today would be within a block of Seabreeze Boulevard. The trolley, very popular at the time, was a transitional mode of transportation between the horse and carriage and the automobile then appearing on the street.

Ruth Law, aviatrix, and Mrs. Robert Goelet, her companion, flew this biplane off the beach and landed it on the beach, Daytona Beach's first landing strip or airport.

The U.S. Army Aviation Section trained pilots at Carlstrom and Dorr fields near Arcadia. Later they had training flights in Daytona Beach, making beach landings. Several pilots were lost in training. This Jenny plane in the tree illustrates the kinds of crashes that befell pilots.

Gene Johnson's fishing and tackle store was on North Beach Street at Fairview. He sold all types of sportsmen's supplies including bicycles. In this image, Koert DuBois demonstrates the advertising bicycle for Johnson.

Beachgoers of the day frequently wore white, the idea being that white shed the most heat. Automobiles were now the vehicle of choice for those of means, who drove and parked on the beach to see and be seen, as persons of prominence in the community. Beach houses are visible in the distance.

This party of DeLand revelers spends a holiday at the beach. The two cars are parked peculiarly and these heavily clothed fun seekers appear to be looking for a coin in the sand. Perhaps they had heard of buried treasure.

William Usher Norwood was well known throughout Volusia County. He is pictured here in his Coast Line office reading railroad schedules for the railroad traffic north and south. Pigeonhole desks like this one were used by most workers before World War I.

Charles G. Burgoyne had the promenade constructed leading all the way from the casino on the corner of Beach and Orange streets to his home at Beach and Bay streets. The seawall, sidewalk, and street lights along Beach Street were all provided by Burgoyne and his wife.

The Pepper family was well known and was active in the Jewish synagogue. Mr. Pepper sold new and used plumbing supplies and also store fixtures. Leonard, sitting at left on the car's running board, attended the University of Florida and became a lawyer and Assistant Attorney General. He owned a large shopping center and other properties in Tallahassee.

Two men and five women stand in the surf with the waves lapping at their knees. It would appear they are afraid to go into deeper water. Bathing suits at this time were mostly made from wool fabric, but light canvas was added to give more of a decorative look. Sometimes men used their undershirts above their swimming trunks. The ladies wore rubber bathing caps to keep their hair dry.

The river width north of Daytona Beach was excellent for landing and taxiing seaplanes to the shore. In later years it became Raymond's Seaplane Base and is known today as Holly Hill. Charles Burgoyne's boathouse was moved to Holly Hill after his death, part of which is seen here down the river. In this image, observers have watched Captain Charles H. Hermann, just arrived from Palm Beach, land his seaplane.

Indian motorcycles were very popular for speeding down the beach, which at low tide was an excellent area for driving vehicles at top speed. The outgoing tide packed the sand, creating a hard surface that prevented wheels from slipping. A typical way to get noticed was for the passenger to stand on the running board of a car.

Ralph DePalma and his car with admirers. His car featured a Packard V-12 engine based on the World War I Liberty aircraft engine, both of which were developed by the Packard engineer Colonel Jesse G. Vincent. DePalma raced through the measured mile at 149.875 M.P.H., which set a new world record February 12, 1919.

Pilots landed their planes on the packed sands at Daytona Beach. These planes flew in from Carlstrom Field, near Arcadia. They parked south of the pier where tourists and local folks could take a look at new models, such as the new U.S. Army Air Service planes.

Real Estate Boom, Depression, and World War II

(1919–1945)

Ervin Ballough (standing), pilot, and Alfred Borden, New York banker and passenger, made this trip to Daytona, the first land-based flight. The plane was a Canuck-Curtiss Jenny, built in Canada.

At center in this aerial view are the Halifax River Yacht Club and city docks. To the right is City Island Ball Field and the city library. Other buildings are the Burgoyne Casino and the business block from Orange Avenue to Volusia Avenue including the concrete bridge.

A typical scene on the beach and near the surf, from early days to the present. The pier provided shade from the sun when desired. For the more ardent, fishing and enjoying the beach could be pursued in the same day. The ocean pier pictured was later rebuilt.

In the days pictured here, Daytona had no mainland airport. The beach served as the landing strip. In view here are various modes of transportation: auto, airplane, and bicycle. The Clarendon Hotel is visible in the distance.

St. Mary's Episcopal Church included beautiful stained-glass windows. The church was to have been named St. Mark's, but in 1883 the cornerstone arrived with "St. Mary's" engraved on it, a mistake the congregation excused.

Left to right are Bob Green in his Fronty-Ford; Bob Putnam, Simplex; Pop Daily, Deusenberg; Sig Haugdahl, Miller Special. Sig Haugdahl later made his home in Daytona. In the rear are eager want-to-be racers.

These men volunteered for the honor of service in the home guards, the frontline of defense in Daytona and the home state. Some were Spanish-American War veterans and many had served in World War I. The home guard was forerunner of the Florida State Guard and the Florida National Guard.

William Usher Norwood and family. This well-known Volusia County resident and his family are being photographed on the beach in their Sunday best, Junior sporting his sailor's suit.

Mable Cody's daredevils thrill the crowds. While Bugs McGowan pulls himself up to hover on the lower wing of the plane, Sig Haugdahl, an experienced race car driver, paces alongside.

Men use land-clearing equipment to prepare streets and create building sites for future houses. Mediterranean Revival, featuring stucco walls and red-tile roofs, was a style typical of the day for building houses.

Pictured is Sig Haugdahl's Wisconsin Special. Haugdahl, probably one of the most experienced race car drivers at that time, was the first man to reach 180 M.P.H., on the beach April 7, 1922.

The Curtiss Oriole was a plane used in many daredevil maneuvers. In back are, left to right, stuntmen Bill Lindley, Glenn E. Messer, Steve Crane, and Gustav Slim Ekstrom. In front, left to right, Jimmy Johnson, Joe Wilson, and Joe Nichols. These men would gain fame for their risky exploits.

A Daytona Highland race car entry, promoted by the Highlands subdivision owners. Many racing events were held on the beach, some of them known as barrel and pillar racing. Smaller race cars were used for special events.

Margaret Biven Haugdahl was the wife of a Daytona sportsman and race car driver. Tarpon fishing was a popular sport and contests were often held for the largest fish. Whether she could have reeled in this big fish with the rod and tackle shown merits scrutiny.

This Mediterranean Revival–style home with its red barrel roof tile was a favorite among home designers. Sales people heavily promoted these new houses at the Highlands subdivision, a prestigious place to live adjacent Daytona.

Children in costume help promote the beautiful facades of Highlands houses during the peak of the real estate boom. Shown here is a replica of one of the facades, built by Daytona Highlands as part of a contest for which the prize was one of the new houses.

The Hotel Morgan, built in 1906, was a luxurious hotel. It was located on the southeast side of Palmetto and Volusia avenues. It had elevators, interspring mattresses, steam heat, and a family-style restaurant. The Greentree Inn and Gables Hotel were next door to the east.

What better way to promote the climate and the beach at Daytona than with beautiful girls and a thermometer.

Hotels and businesses line Volusia Avenue. The Gables Hotel, the Greentree Inn, and Morgan Hotel were on the south side, known as Hotel Row. Several small businesses including a barbershop operated at street level under the Greentree Inn.

A policeman directs traffic on the beach as beachgoers gather for a gala occasion. The Clarendon Hotel can be seen to the north, with other smaller hotels nearby.

Yachts lie anchored on the south side of the Halifax Yacht Club. From time to time these pleasure craft moored in the basin.

Beauty contests were an attraction advertising the businesses of the Halifax area. These seven contestants are hoping to take first place. The Daytona Beach Pier was a landmark recognized throughout the country.

Three days after Kaye Don tried to break the speed record traveling over 190 M.P.H. through the measured mile, crowds gather again to see the competition of cars. This early concrete walk, which later became the WPA boardwalk, was a favorite place to view the start of the time trials. This photograph was taken from the Ocean Pier.

Kaye Don and his Sunbeam Silver Bullet Race Car. This was the longest race car to appear on the beach to run through the measured mile. At 31 feet long, it had rear stabilizing fins, two supercharged V-12 Sunbeam engines, and the driving compartment sat over the rear wheels. Don failed to reach the projected speed.

Charles G. Burgoyne died in 1916, but he left a legacy of tourist diversions, including the Burgoyne Shuffleboard Club pictured here. Competition took place on the mainland and the peninsula. Other recreational games, such as lawn bowling, were played near the Beach Street Burgoyne Casino.

Dave Sholtz campaigns in the summer of 1932 for governor of Florida. Beach Street was always crowded for political rallies. Sholtz's law office was on Beach Street, and he was well known throughout the city.

David Sholtz and his wife, Alice May. This couple worked very hard campaigning for the governorship of Florida. Always well dressed with his familiar Palm Beach strawhat, Sholtz traveled throughout Central Florida as the democratic candidate for this office.

Mr. Strapp worked two clandestine years in Paris, France, to build this race car. He claimed 300 M.P.H. on the Daytona sands were possible. The car appears to be designed for speed, but he was unable to substantiate his claims.

Fun and sun were reason enough for an outing on the beach. These young people, in bathing suits more like those of today than of earlier times, are ready for a brace of ocean air and bravery in the surf.

Captain J. Kershaw flew a National Airlines plane—a single engine Ryan. He made the first flight from Daytona Beach to St. Petersburg on October 15, 1934. Like many pilots, he also carried U.S. mail.

The Federal Emergency Relief Administration assisted with funds to build this shuffleboard court near the baseball field. In the distance the new fire station can be seen. To the left the Halifax River Yacht Club and boat shelter are visible.

A Florida East Coast passenger train, headed up by a Flagler diesel locomotive, pulls streamlined coaches and Pullman cars. Each winter in this era tourists from the north traveled on these trains to sunny Florida.

The Daytona Beach Bandshell was a federal Work Projects Administration project funded through tax dollars. With benches of concrete and wood, this large outdoor theater featured coquina rock walls enclosing the seating area.

This casino, a landmark along Beach Street, was built by Charles G. Burgoyne, who died in 1916. The photograph was taken from City Island depicting the back view of the casino. Shown are the veranda and gazebo, which were used by tourists and local citizens.

These cars bear the school colors during the Bethune-Cookman College 41st Anniversary celebration.
Mary McLeod Bethune was very proud of the accomplishments that had been made.

In this view north from the Bandshell tower, picnic shelters and umbrella trees are visible. This area was maintained as a park, and at high tide locals and tourists could park their cars on the street behind the bandshell.

World War II was over and once again the beach was a playground for tourists. Left to right, Shirley Ostroff of Boston and Peggy Devers of Norfolk are enjoying a drive on the beach. These electric cars were a profitable rental service.

GROWTH, THE BEACH, TOURISM, AND RACING

(1946–1949)

Some tourists, then as now, came to Daytona Beach to enjoy the beach and some came to enjoy the fishing. Nannie Boaz of Nashville, Tennessee, catches a 40-pound sailfish over six feet long, several miles out on a party boat. Fishing tournaments were held each year in the Daytona Beach area.

Beach trams have always been popular on day and night tours. Often tram drivers would pick up the passengers at the hotels, motels, and near the boardwalk. The price of the tour pictured here was 25 cents a person.

Looking south from the bandshell, the south wall of the outdoor theater can be seen. Farther south are concessions and to the right the clock tower. On the left in the distance is the ocean pier.

Robert Byron was one of the most colorful drivers after World War II. Fans gave him the name Boss of the Beach. Passing other cars in the turns, he would come into the north turn so fast his vehicle was turned sideways. He won four races.

Gil Ferrell serves as flag man to open stock car races on the beach. With roaring engines, the cars headed for the north turn. Photographers were eager to see who would take the lead.

Bob Flock—in race car no. 14—leaves the north turn as another racer pursues. Race drivers put on a show for the fans at this turn, with spinning tires throwing marl and sand. The Flock brothers were favorites at the 3.5-mile road-beach course.

Left to right are Bill France, Sr., race director, and Robert Byron, race driver. Byron accepted the
Edward Knowles Rayson Memorial Trophy (cup) for winning the January 26, 1947, race. Red Vogt
built the 39 Ford race car in 48 hours.

The marker pretty well speaks for itself: On this beach, along the Measured Mile, over the course of time, racers set 80 world automobile speed records. The sign stood on the beach near the Dunlawton Beach approach. Sir Malcolm Campbell was the last racer to break the world's land speed record, setting a new record of 276.82 M.P.H.

Young people are creative with their beach games. Here playing leapfrog are four youngsters, photographed on Armistice Day, November 11, 1948.

This boat works had a dry dock and large machine shop area. Here boats could be overhauled with new planking, siding, and other needed repairs. New gasoline or diesel engines could be replaced inside the craft on new engine beds.

Over time, tourist facilities on the beach were growing larger. The names of tourist houses, courts, and cabins were changing. This new facility called its resort a Colony. Entertainment (recreation) on the beachfront was added.

The Flamingo Shoe Company plant was located in a former Navy building. At the time this photograph was taken, very few buildings offered air conditioning for their employees. Workers are shown here with short sleeves or no shirts at their work tables.

Henry Pierce teaches six young visitors on the beach the skills of sand sailing. This three-wheeled sailing craft could be dangerous in strong winds; without a breeze, it sat motionless. Tacking was the name of the game to operate the land-sailor successfully.

A huge crowd convenes at the bandshell for a special program and beauty contest. Participants came from nearby cities. There were age limits and strict rules for those who entered the contest.

July 4th has always been a special day on the beach. This photograph was taken from the pier. Visible are peanut shelters in front of the boardwalk, a huge crowd, Ferris wheel, the clock tower, and the bandshell. Sun bathers enjoy the beach sand and surf.

Pictured here on the sands of Daytona are seven young ladies and a lifeguard. In the background are a number of motels and apartment buildings.

In this view from times gone by, beachgoers enjoy the boardwalk, beach, and ocean pier. At night, fireworks were set off at the end of the pier. Visitors with cars on the beach have always been alert to an incoming tide; when parking was permitted on the beach, the risk of saltwater seeping into one's car was ever-present.

In this view, girls involved in the beauty pageant are being instructed in their role in the contest while the musical director plans his part of the program.

Notes on the Photographs

These notes, listed by page number, attempt to include all aspects known of the photographs. Each of the photographs is identified by the page number, a title or description, photographer and collection, archive, and call or box number when applicable. Although every attempt was made to collect all data, in some cases complete data may have been unavailable due to the age and condition of some of the photographs and records.

II BEACH RACING
Florida State Archives
rc13545

VI FERDINAND THE BULL
Florida State Archives
pr02298

X 145 SOUTH BEACH STREET
Florida State Archives
rc08576

2 STEAM LOCOMOTIVE
Florida State Archives
rc6067

3 OCEAN BOULEVARD
Florida State Archives
rc06727

4 RIDGEWOOD AVENUE
Florida State Archives
no34716

5 DEVELOPING BEACHSIDE
Florida State Archives
rc9728

6 YACHT CLUB
Florida State Archives
rc16391

7 KEARING PIER
Florida State Archives
rc9170

8 YACHT CLUB AND PIER
Florida State Archives
rc16409

9 FIRST CAR IN DAYTONA
Florida State Archives
rc16410

10 SOUTH BRIDGE
Florida State Archives
rc7626

11 PALMETTO HOUSE
Florida State Archives
rc13165

12 BEACH RIDING
Florida State Archives
rc7068

13 JITNEY
Florida State Archives
rc05157

14 DUBOIS' WIFE ON BEACH
Florida State Archives
no38250

15 SOUTH BEACH STREET
Florida State Archives
no31177

16 ENGINEERING CONVENTION
Florida State Archives
no29824

17 WOODEN PIER
Florida State Archives
cc297

18 RAIL STATION
Florida State Archives
rc04352

19 OPERA HOUSE
Florida State Archives
rc16371

20 OCEAN BOULEVARD
Florida State Archives
rc9056

21 TREE LINED AVENUE
Florida State Archives
pr02323

22 THE "DIXIE"
Florida State Archives
rc6943

23 BURDINE'S PHARMACY
Florida State Archives
rc6949

24 THE "CHEROKEE"
Florida State Archives
rc16390

25 THE "UNCLE SAM"
Florida State Archives
rc4761

26 CITY ISLAND
Florida State Archives
rc9057

27 BEACH VISITORS
Florida State Archives
rc02758

28 SPORT SPECTATORS
Florida State Archives
rc-063

29 BURGOYNE MANSION
Florida State Archives
rc12466

30 PUBLIC LIBRARY
Florida State Archives
rc13167

31 TO THE SAWMILL
Florida State Archives
rc02742

32 BEACH RACE
Florida State Archives
rc7071

33 BETHUNE'S STUDENTS
Florida State Archives
no41432

34 BEACH STREET
Florida State Archives
rc16361

35 MACDONALD'S RACE CAR
Florida State Archives
rc5327

36 HOTEL DESPLAND
Florida State Archives
rc4705

37 TURPENTINE
Florida State Archives
cc897

38 MAIN STREET BRIDGE
Florida State Archives
rc7521

40 GENERATIONS ON BEACH
Florida State Archives
rc13501

41 ORGAN GRINDER
Florida State Archives
rc13652

42 NEW GENERATOR
Florida State Archives
rc7651

43 BEACHED WHALES
Florida State Archives
rc12083

44 WINTER INN
Florida State Archives
no29837

45 ROXANA
Florida State Archives
no40786

46 RIDGEWOOD AVENUE
Florida State Archives
pr02326

47 FUTURE STREET PIER
Florida State Archives
rc16367

48 CROWDED DEPOT
Florida State Archives
pr02328

49 HOTCHKISS RACER
Florida State Archives
rc10417

50 FIRE DISASTER
Florida State Archives
no31169

51 WOOL SUIT BATHERS
Florida State Archives
pr02333

52 LADIES ON THE BEACH
Florida State Archives
pr0233

53 FUTURE LOOMIS STREET
Florida State Archives
no29878

54 HALIFAX YACHT CLUB
Florida State Archives
rc16373

55 BAND ENTERTAINMENT
Florida State Archives
rc13174

56 CURTISS' AIRCRAFT
Florida State Archives
rc11256

57 HALIFAX RIVER FERRY
Florida State Archives
rc16389

58 FIRST HALIFAX BRIDGE
Florida State Archives
no28462

59 ELKS CLUBHOUSE
Florida State Archives
no29500

60 **BETHUNE IN FAITH HALL**
Florida State Archives
pr000796

61 **DAYTONA TROLLEY**
Florida State Archives
rc07701

62 **MISS LAW'S FLIGHT**
Florida State Archives
rc7964

63 **JENNY PLANE CRASH**
Florida State Archives
rc12767

64 **JOHNSON'S BICYCLE**
Florida State Archives
rc13498

65 **BEACHGOERS**
Florida State Archives
no29468

66 **TWO CARS ON BEACH**
Florida State Archives
no29478

67 **NORWOOD'S OFFICE**
Florida State Archives
no29860

68 **BURGOYNE'S SEASIDE**
Florida State Archives
no29818

69 **PEPPER FAMILY**
Florida State Archives
ms25322

70 **GROUP IN THE SURF**
Florida State Archives
no29482

71 **SEAPLANES**
Florida State Archives
pr00480

72 **INDIAN MOTORCYCLES**
Florida State Archives
pr13972

73 **DEPALMA**
Florida State Archives
no41916

74 **PLANES ON BEACH**
Florida State Archives
no27962

76 **TRIP TO DAYTONA**
Florida State Archives
no27964

77 **HALIFAX RIVER**
Florida State Archives
rc12467

78 **PEOPLE NEAR THE PIER**
Florida State Archives
ms25317

79 **DAYTONA AIRPORT**
Florida State Archives
no27976

80 **SAINT MARY'S**
Florida State Archives
pr02321

81 **BEACH RACERS**
Florida State Archives
no41974

82 **FLORIDA STATE GUARD**
Florida State Archives
no313198

83 **NORWOOD'S FAMILY**
Florida State Archives
no42734

84 **CODY'S DAREDEVILS**
Florida State Archives
rc12187

85 **CLEARING THE LAND**
Florida State Archives
no29844

86 **WISCONSIN SPECIAL**
Florida State Archives
no41959

87 **THE CURTIS ORIOLE**
Florida State Archives
rc15183

88 **HIGHLANDS RACE CAR**
Florida State Archives
no41940

89 **TARPON FISHING**
Florida State Archives
no29854

90 **HIGHLANDS SUBDIVISION**
Florida State Archives
no29871

91 **HIGHLANDS PROMOTION**
Florida State Archives
no9850

92 **HOTEL MORGAN**
Florida State Archives
rc16396

93 **BEACH CLIMATE**
Florida State Archives
no28823

94 **VOLUSIA AVENUE**
Florida State Archives
rc16397

95 **BEACH TRAFFIC**
Florida State Archives
no29480

96 **HALIFAX YACHT CLUB**
Florida State Archives
no29872

97 **BEAUTY CONTEST**
Florida State Archives
no28821

98 **KAYE DON'S ATTEMPT**
Florida State Archives
rc00270

99 **SILVER BULLET**
Florida State Archives
rc10436

100 **SHUFFLEBOARD CLUB**
Florida State Archives
no29496

101 SHOLTZ CAMPAIGN
Florida State Archives
no27176

102 SHOLTZ AND HIS WIFE
Florida State Archives
no27158

103 MR. STRAPP
Florida State Archives
pr14099

104 YOUNG PEOPLE ON
BEACH
Florida State Archives
pr02310

105 NATIONAL AIRLINES
Florida State Archives
rc4827

106 SHUFFLEBOARD CLUB
Florida State Archives
pr02341

107 PASSENGER TRAIN
Florida State Archives
rc29858

108 BEACH BANDSHELL
Florida State Archives
ge1827

109 CASINO ON BEACH
STREET
Florida State Archives
rc16386

110 PARADE OF CARS
Florida State Archives
pr0774

111 BEACH PARK
Florida State Archives
c005379

112 ELECTRIC BEACH CARS
Florida State Archives
c005377

114 SAILFISH
Florida State Archives
c06313

115 BEACH TRAMS
Florida State Archives
c005346

116 SOUTH WALL
Florida State Archives
c005381

117 BOSS OF THE BEACH
Florida State Archives
c002640

118 GIL FERRELL
Florida State Archives
c002655

119 BOB FLOCK
Florida State Archives
c002647

120 RAYSON MEMORIAL
TROPHY
Florida State Archives
c002641

121 MEASURED MILE BOARD
Florida State Archives
c002677

122 ARMISTICE DAY
Florida State Archives
c006680

123 MACHINE SHOP AREA
Florida State Archives
c10710

124 COLONY RESORTS
Florida State Archives
c10425

125 FLAMINGO SHOE CO.
Florida State Archives
c10704

126 HENRY PIERCE
Florida State Archives
c11338

127 BEAUTY CONTEST
Florida State Archives
c007898

128 JULY 4TH
Florida State Archives
c11277

129 LIFEGUARD STAND
Florida State Archives
c11328

130 BEACHGOERS
Florida State Archives
c11238

131 BEAUTY PAGEANT
Florida State Archives
c11301

Printed in the USA
CPSIA information can be obtained
at www.ICGtesting.com
JSHW072024140824
68134JS00042B/3768